Inkscape 0.48 Starter

Get started with this quick introduction to Inkscape,
its features, and the community

Bethany Hiitola

PUBLISHING

BIRMINGHAM - MUMBAI

Inkscape Starter

First published: September 2011

Production Reference: 1050811

Published by Packt Publishing Ltd.
Livery Place
35 Livery Street
Birmingham B3 2PB, UK.

ISBN 978-1-849517-56-0

www.packtpub.com

www.PacktPub.com

Support files, eBooks, discount offers and more

You might want to visit www.PacktPub.com for support files and downloads related to your book.

Did you know that Packt offers eBook versions of every book published, with PDF and ePub files available? You can upgrade to the eBook version at www.PacktPub.com and as a print book customer, you are entitled to a discount on the eBook copy. Get in touch with us at service@packtpub.com for more details.

At www.PacktPub.com, you can also read a collection of free technical articles, sign up for a range of free newsletters and receive exclusive discounts and offers on Packt books and eBooks.

http://PacktLib.PacktPub.com

www.PacktLib.PacktPub.com

Do you need instant solutions to your IT questions? PacktLib is Packt's online digital book library. Here, you can access, read and search across Packt's entire library of books.

Why Subscribe?

- ✦ Fully searchable across every book published by Packt
- ✦ Copy and paste, print and bookmark content
- ✦ On demand and accessible via web browser

Free Access for Packt account holders

If you have an account with Packt at www.PacktPub.com, you can use this to access PacktLib today and view nine entirely free books. Simply use your login credentials for immediate access.

Table of Contents

Inkscape Starter

Welcome to the Inkscape Starter. Here you'll learn the basics of Inkscape, get started with a few basic vector graphic projects, and discover some tips and tricks for using Inkscape.

This document contains the following sections:

So what is Inkscape? – find out what Inkscape actually is, what you can do with it, and why it's so great.

What are vector graphics? – understand what vector graphics are and the characteristics that make them invaluable in web and print design.

Installation – learn how to download and install Inkscape with the minimum fuss and then set it up so that you can use it as soon as possible.

Quick start—this section will show you how to perform one of the core tasks of Inkscape; building vector graphics. Follow the steps to create your own vector graphic, which will be the basis of most of your work in Inkscape.

Top features you need to know about – here you will learn how to perform seven tasks with the most important features in Inkscape. By the end of this section you will be able to use paths and layers, combine shapes, create and edit text tools, and import and embed images.

People and places you should get to know – every Open Source project is centered around a community. This section provides you with many useful links to the project page and forums, as well as a number of helpful articles, tutorials, blogs and the Twitter feeds of Inkscape super-contributors.

This document was written to Inkscape version 0.48

So, what is Inkscape?

Inkscape is an Open Source, free program that creates vector-based graphics that can be used in web, print, and screen design as well as interface and logo creation, and material cutting. Its capabilities are similar to those of commercial products such as Adobe Illustrator, Macromedia Freehand, and CorelDraw and it can be used for any number of practical purposes—creating vector graphics for use in illustrations, business letterheads, computer and electronic wallpapers, designing logos, and—as is the focus of this book—designing web pages and the elements within web page design.

You not only get a free download under the GNU General Public License (GPL), but can use the program to create items with it and freely distribute them, modify the program itself, and share that modified program with others.

Inkscape uses **Scalable Vector Graphics** (**SVG**), a vector-based drawing language that uses some basic principles:

+ A drawing can (and should) be scalable to any size without losing detail
+ A drawing can use an unlimited number of smaller drawings used (and reused) in any number of ways and still be a part of a larger whole

SVG and World Wide Web Consortium (W3C) web standards are built into Inkscape, giving it a number of features including a rich body of XML (eXtensible Markup Language) format with complete descriptions and animations.

Inkscape drawings can be reused in other SVG-compliant drawing programs and can adapt to different presentation methods. It has support across most web browsers (Firefox, Chrome, Opera, Safari, and Internet Explorer).

When you draw your objects (rectangles, circles, and so on), arbitrary paths, and text in Inkscape, you also give them attributes such as color, gradient, or patterned fills. Inkscape automatically creates a web mark up (XML) for each of these elements. If need be, the graphics can then be transformed, cloned, and grouped in the code itself. Hyperlinks can even be added for use in web browsers, multi-lingual scripting (which isn't available in most commercial vector-based programs) and more—all within Inkscape or in a native programming language. It makes your vector graphics more versatile in the web space than a standard JPG or GIF graphic.

There are still some limitations in the Inkscape program, even though it aims to be fully SVG compliant. For example, as of version 0.48 it still does not support animation or the full SVG specification.

What are vector graphics?

Vector graphics are made up of paths. Each path is basically a line with a start and end point, curves, angles, and points that are calculated with a mathematical equation. These paths are not limited to being straight—they can be of any shape, size, and even encompass any number of curves. When you combine them, they create drawings, diagrams, and can even help create certain fonts.

These characteristics make vector graphics very different than JPEGs, GIFs, or BMP images—all of which are considered rasterized or bitmap images made up of tiny squares which are called pixels or bits. If you magnify these images, you will see they are made up of a grid (bitmaps) and if you keep magnifying them, they will become blurry and grainy as each pixel with bitmap square's zoom level grows larger.

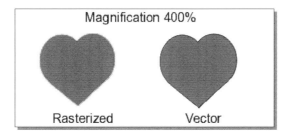

Computer monitors also use pixels in a grid. However, they use millions of them so that when you look at a display, your eyes see a picture. In high-resolution monitors, the pixels are smaller and closer together to give a crisper image.

How does this all relate to vector-based graphics? Vector-based graphics aren't made up of squares. Since they are based on paths, you can make them larger (by scaling) and the image quality stays the same, lines and edges stay clean, and the same images can be used on items as small as letterheads or business cards or blown up to be billboards or used in high definition animation sequences. This flexibility, often accompanied by smaller file sizes, makes vector graphics ideal—especially in the world of the Internet, varying computer displays, and hosting services for web spaces, which leads us nicely to Inkscape, a tool that can be invaluable for use designing for both web and print.

If you are new to design, you might be surprised to learn that even when you are using a word processing program, you are using vector graphics all the time—fonts! Fonts, are objects that are grouped together to make the shape of letters and illustrate the behaviors of all vector graphics.

✦ An entire font with all its letters, numbers, and symbols is a very small file size.
✦ Fonts can be set to any size without losing quality.

Some vector-based applications allow you convert text to paths so you can modify the shapes of the letters themselves.

Installation

In three easy steps, you can install Inkscape 0.48 and get it set up on your system.

1 – What do I need?

Inkscape is available for download for Windows, Macintosh, Linux, or Solaris operating systems. Before you install Inkscape, you will need to check that you have all of the required elements, as listed below:

✦ Operating system: Windows Me, NT, or XP and Vista. Mac OS X version 10.3 (Panther) or higher. Most Linux distributions are supported.

✦ Disk space: A minimum of 200MB free. More free space is required to store your graphics projects.

✦ Inkscape requires an internet connection if you plan to use the Open Clip Art Library.

> To run on the Mac OS X operating system, Inkscape typically runs under X11—an implementation of the X Window System software that makes it possible to run X11-based applications in Mac OS X. The X11 application has shipped with the Mac OS X since version 10.5.
>
> When you open Inkscape on a Mac, it will first open X11 and run Inkscape within that program. Loss of some shortcut key options will occur but all functionality is present using menus and toolbars.

2 – Downloading Inkscape

Go to the official Inkscape website at: `http://www.inkscape.org/` and download the appropriate version of the software for your computer.

For the Mac OS X Leopard software, you will also need to download an additional application. It is the X11 application package 2.4.0 or greater from this website: `http://xquartz.macosforge.org/trac/wiki/X112.4.0`.

Once downloaded, double-click the `X11-2.4.0.DMG` package first. It will open another folder with the X11 application installer. Double-click that icon to be prompted through an installation wizard.

3 – Installing Inkscape

Double-click the downloaded Inkscape installation package to start the installation.

For the Mac OS, a DMG file is downloaded. Double-click on it and then drag and drop the Inkscape package to the Application Folder.

For any Windows device, a `.exe` file is downloaded. Double-click that file to start and complete the installation.

For Linux-based computers, there are a number of distributions available. Be sure to download and install the correct installation package for your system.

Now find the Inkscape icon in the **Application** or **Programs** folders to open the program:

Double-click the Inkscape icon and the program will automatically open to the main screen:

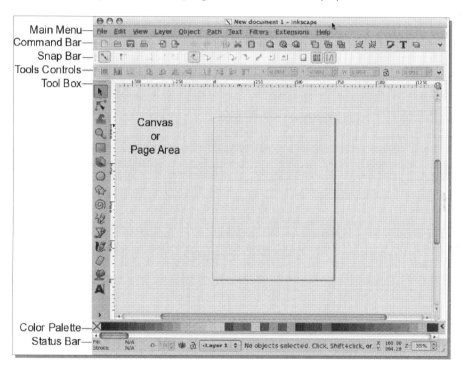

And that's it!!

By this point, you should have a working installation of Inkscape 0.48 and are free to play around and discover more about it.

Quick start—Creating your first vector graphic

Vector graphics are made up of paths. Each path is basically a line with a start and end point, curves, angles, and points that are calculated with a mathematical equation. These paths are not limited to being straight—they can be of any shape, size, and even encompass any number of curves. When you combine them, they create drawings, diagrams, and can even help create certain fonts.

Inkscape uses both paths and a series of pre-determined shapes when creating graphics. Paths have no pre-defined lengths or widths. They are arbitrary in nature and come in three basic types:

✦ Open paths (have two ends)

✦ Closed paths (have no ends, like a circle)

✦ Compound paths (use a combination of two open and/or closed paths)

In Inkscape there are a few ways we can make paths; with the Pencil (Freehand), Bezier (Pen), and Calligraphy tools—all of which are found in the tool box, which is located at the side of your screen.

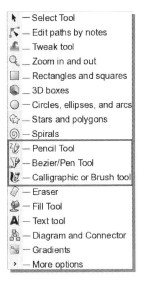

They can also be created by converting a regular shape or text object into paths.

In general, we use paths to build unique objects that aren't part of the SVG standard shapes in Inkscape. Since we can combine paths and make them closed objects—they again can be resized, manipulated, and then exported in a number of formats.

In this section, we will show you how to create some basic vector graphics with shapes and paths in Inkscape (which thankfully, doesn't require you to do any mathematical equations when using it) and export them in a couple of different formats.

1 – Opening a new document

As stated when you first open Inkscape, a new document is opened and ready to start. However, it uses a default canvas size of 8.5in x 11in (standard letter size) and you may need to change orientations and sizes for a graphic you are creating.

1. Select **File | New**. A menu appears with the many pre-defined sizes Inkscape has for you.

2. Choose one and a new document opens with the specified size.

3. If you want to manually change your document properties just go to the main menu and select **File | Document Properties**. You'll see the **Document Properties** window displayed with a number of options for customizing your canvas and "printable" page.

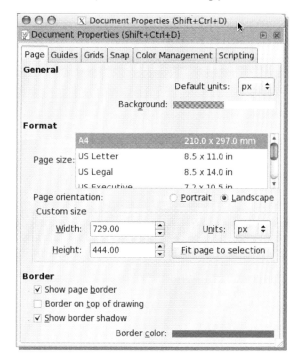

2 – Creating shapes

Inkscape can also create shapes that are part of the SVG standard. These include: rectangles/ squares, circles/ellipses/arcs, stars, polygons, and spirals. To create any of these shapes, do the following:

1. Select (click) the shape tool icon in the tool box, as highlighted in the screenshot below.

2. Then draw the shape on the canvas by clicking, holding, and then dragging the shape to the size you want on the canvas:

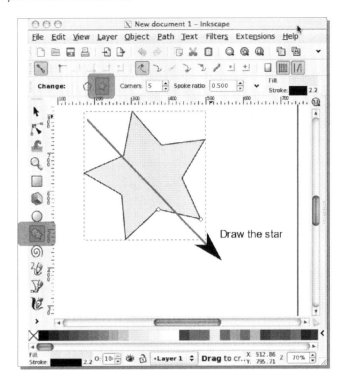

3. To switch between creating stars and polygons, select that star/polygon icon in the tool box on the left-hand side of your screen, and then select either the polygon or the star icon in the Tool controls (just above the canvas).

3 – Changing shape options

Shapes have a number of attributes or options that are assigned to them. In Inkscape, the user interface gives you easy tools to change options such as fill color, stroke color, size, and placement of the shape.

1. Change the fill color of the shape by selecting a color in the color palette:

2. Change the stroke or border color by pressing and holding the *Shift* key and then selecting that color from the color palette.

3. Change the position of the shape on the canvas by choosing the Select tool in the tool box, clicking and holding the shape, and moving it where you need it to be:

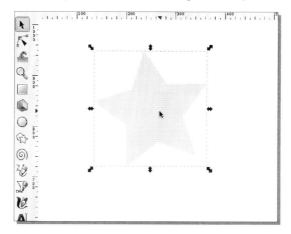

4. Change the size of the shape by also choosing the Select tool from the tool box, clicking and holding the edge of the shape at the node (small square or circles at edges), and dragging it outward to grow larger or inward to shrink until the shape is of the desired size.

4 – Saving your graphic

1. Inkscape will, by default, save projects in its default format, SVG. To do this, you click **File | Save**.

2. However, you might also want to export in a bitmap graphic format like PNG. To do this, choose **File | Export Bitmap**.

3. In the **Export Bitmap** window, you can choose to save the **Page** (all objects), the **Drawing**, the **Selection** (only the object you have selected), or customize it.

4. Choose the **Export area**, the graphic size you want (will select pre-defined size by default), and click **Browse** to choose the same location.

5. Verify the file name in the text box and click **Export**.

6. To save in another format besides PNG, go to **File | Save As** and choose the file format of your choice. Inkscape allows you to save in a number of formats such as: PDF, EPS, ODG, WMF, and others. However, remember that if you want to save the file in a format that will allow you to edit in the future, you need to save it in Inkscape SVG.

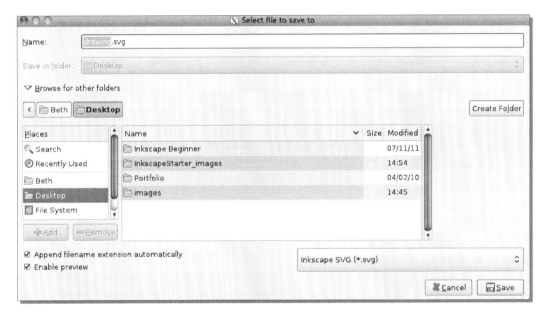

Top features you'll want to know about

As you start to use Inkscape, you will realize that there are a wide variety of things that you can do with it. This section will teach you all about the most commonly performed tasks and most commonly used features in Inkscape.

1 – Using paths

You can also use the Bezier (Pen) Tool to create objects in a bit more of a freehand form. This tool allows you to create straight lines and curves and connect them to create a freehand object. Here's an example of how to create a lightning bolt:

1. From a new document, choose the Bezier Pen tool from the tool box:

2. Click somewhere on the canvas to start drawing a straight line; click to establish a node. Click again to change the direction of the straight line to create an angle in our lightning bolt:

    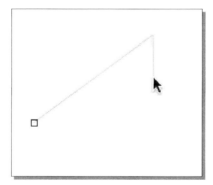

3. Continue to create the lightning bolt object by joining line segments.

4. Don't worry if you stop a line and realize you need to extend its length. Just drag a straight line to add on to the original to make it as long as you need. Click again when you are ready to change directions.

5. Also, if you made a mistake, there's no need to start over. Press the *Backspace* or *Delete* key and it removes the last line segment.

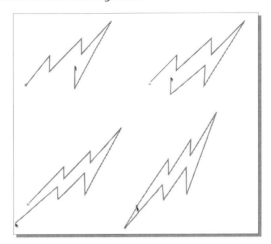

6. To "close" the lightning bolt, just create a line segment and join it to the starting point with a final click. You'll see that all of the lines are combined into one continuous closed path—a lightning bolt.

7. When you select the lightning bolt, the entire object is selected. You can resize it, fill it with a color (select it and choose a color from the color palette), and move it to another location on the canvas. It's become a unique object for you to work with.

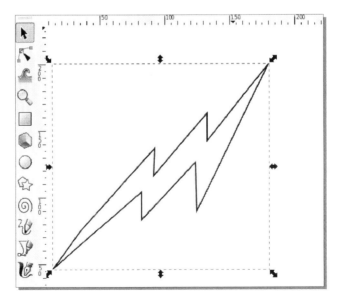

8. Remember, if you want to save this graphic, from the main menu select **File | Save.**

2 – Combining shapes

Sometimes as a designer you are asked to create logos or shapes that are outside the standard ones provided in the software. Since Inkscape is vector-based, you can combine simple shapes, masking, hiding, and layering them to create these more complex shapes. Let's perform an exercise to see how this can be done. We'll create a heart as an example:

1. Open a new document (any size will do, since we are just practicing).

2. Select the Circle/Ellipse tool in the tool box.

3. Create a circle shape:

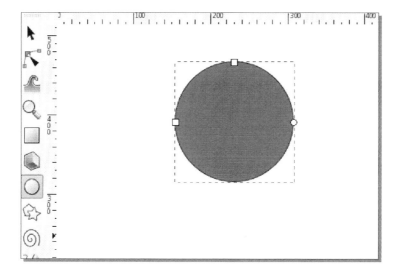

4. On the main menu choose **Edit | Duplicate** or use the keyboard shortcut *Ctrl/Cmd* and *D*.

5. From the tool box, choose the Select tool and then select the topmost circle object (the duplicate) and move that circle to the right side of the first, to make the crest of the heart. Press and hold the *Ctrl* key while you drag the circle to lock the horizontal axes of both circles:

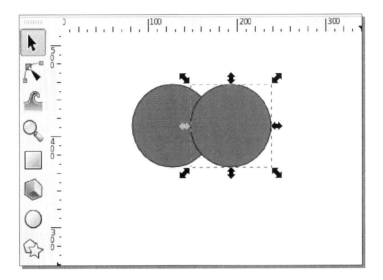

6. From the tool box, choose the Star/Polygon tool.

7. In the Tool Control bar, make sure that the Polygon tool is selected:

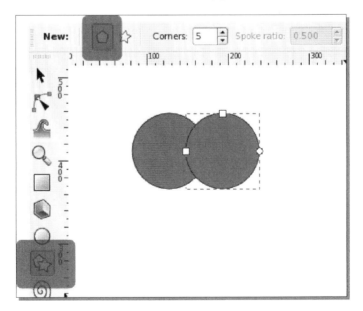

8. Draw a polygon just below the circles on the canvas, with a point facing downward:

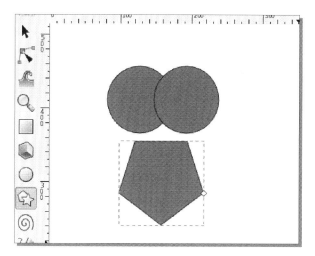

Rotating an object

While drawing the polygon on the canvas, you can swivel it up, down, left, and right to position it with a point downward (for the bottom of the heart).

It is okay if you don't do this while drawing it initially; you can always choose the Select tool from the tool box, and click the polygon until the nodes turn to arrows with curves (this might require you to click the polygon object a couple of times). When you see the curved arrow nodes, click and drag on a corner node to rotate the object until it is positioned correctly.

9. Now choose the Select tool from the tool box, and drag the polygon so it creates the bottom point of the heart:

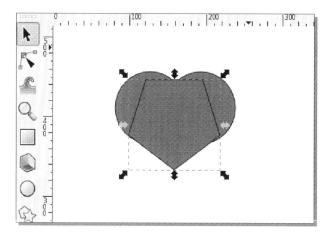

10. To readjust the size of the polygon so that the "top" doesn't ruin the crest of the heart and so that side points align with the sides of the circles, just make sure the Select tool is active, and click the polygon. The resize nodes appear.

11. Click the node on a side that needs to be adjusted and resize it. Repeat this as necessary until the polygon "fits" within the circles correctly:

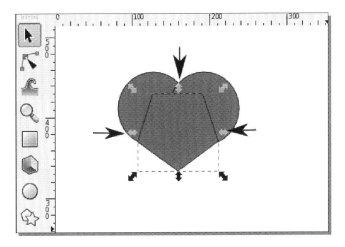

12. With the polygon still selected, press and hold the *Shift* key while you select each circle so all objects are selected.

13. On the main menu select **Path | Union**.

14. This merges all three shapes into one... and voila, it's a heart!

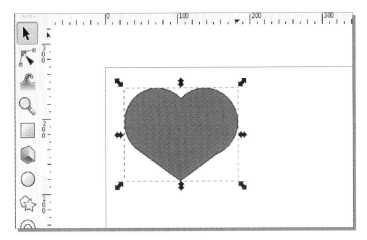

3 – Creating and editing text tools

✦ Creating text in a project is simple—select the Create and Edit Text tool in the tool box, as shown in the image below, click at the insertion point within an open project, and start typing.

✦ The text is immediately displayed on the canvas:

✦ The text tool (the A icon) in the tool box shown above is the only way of creating new text on the canvas. The T icon shown in the Command Bar is used only when editing the text that already exists on the canvas.

✦ You can use the **Text and Font** menu to change everything from the font, style, size, and alignment. To open this window, from the main menu select **Text | Text and Font** (or use the shortcut keys and press *Shift and Ctrl and T*).

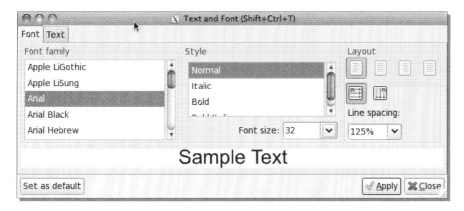

✦ This window dialog also has a unique (and often useful) feature where you can edit your text directly. Click the **Text** tab and select the text you want to change, or add/ delete.

✦ Back in the **Font** tab you can change the font itself, the point size, alignment, line spacing, and even change from horizontal to vertical text layout. But note, even with options for **Bold**, **Italics**, or **Bold Italics** there is no option for **Underline**.

- ✦ You can also change the spacing of a selected text by using shortcut keys. Use the *Alt and* > or *Alt and* < keys to try it out. There are some limitations of these shortcuts with Mac, Linux, and Windows VistaOS versions.

- ✦ You can change the kerning of the font as well. Double-click some text that you have already entered in an open project. This will take you into the **Create and Edit Text** tool allowing you to edit the text letter by letter.

- ✦ Using the arrow keys, move the cursor between the two letters where you want to add or diminish the space between.

- ✦ Then, press the *Alt* and the *Right Arrow* Key to add space between the letters. Or alternatively, press the *Alt and the Left Arrow* Key to lessen the space between those two letters. There are some limitations of these shortcuts with Mac, Linux, and Windows Vista OS versions.

- ✦ Then press *Alt and the Up* Key to move the letter(s) up from the horizontal baseline.

- ✦ Or use the *Alt and the Down* Key combination to move a letter down from the horizontal baseline. There are some limitations of these shortcuts with Mac, Linux, and Windows Vista OS versions.

- ✦ You can even rotate letters. Select a letter you want to rotate left or right and then use the *Alt* and the [or] keys to start moving it.

4 – Text styling keyboard shortcuts

Since not all text styling options are available via a menu item, here's an overview of all the text options via keyboard shortcuts.

> Remember: There are limitations of using shortcuts that contain the *Alt* key with Mac, Linux, and Windows Vista operating systems.

Text Selection Shortcut Keys	
Ctrl + Left/Right Arrows	Cursor moves word by word.
Shift + Left/Right Arrows	Selects/deselects letter by letter.
Ctrl + Shift + Left/Right Arrows	Selects/deselects word by word.
Double click on letters	Selects the word.
Triple click	Selects the entire line of text.
Shift + Home For Mac OS: Shift + Fn + Left Arrow	Selects from the beginning of the line until the cursor position.
Shift + End For Mac OS: Shift + Fn + Right Arrow	Selects from cursor to the end of the line.
Ctrl + Shift + Home For Mac OS: Ctrl + Shift + Fn + Left Arrow	Selects from the beginning of the text until the cursor position.
Ctrl + Shift + End For Mac OS: Ctrl + Shift + Fn + Right Arrow	Selects from the cursor position until the end of the text.
Hot Keys	
Ctrl + B	Applies bold style to the selected text.
Ctrl + I	Applies italic style to the selected text.
Alt + Right or Left Arrows	Increase or decrease the space between characters (kerning).
Alt + > or < keys	Changes the overall letter spacing within that text box.
Alt + [or] keys	Rotates letters.
Alt + Up or Down Arrows	Change the vertical position of the selected text relatively to the baseline.
Alt + Shift + Arrows	Moves position by 10 pixel steps.
Ctrl + [or]	Rotates 90°.

5—Using Drop Shadows and Reflections

One of the most common effects seen with text elements—and one of the easiest to do—is creating a reflection or shadow of the letters in the word. We'll learn how to do both with some example text.

Drop Shadows

Let's work through an example of making a simple drop shadow.

1. Open a new document in Inkscape, Select the Create and Edit Text tool, and enter some text. In our example, we'll use the words: `Darkness and Mystery`

2. With the text selected from the main menu select **Filters**, **Shadows and Glows** and then choose **Drop Shadow**.

3. In the Drop Shadow window, choose settings that work for the drop shadow you want to create. We'll use a Blur radius of 5 pixels, Opacity of 80% and offsets for horizontal and vertical set at 5 pixels.

4. Press **Apply** and the drop shadow will be set.

But there are a lot more filters here that you can use that will give neat effects for your text. These include cutouts, cutout and glow, dark and glow, drop glow, fuzzy glow, glow, in and out, inner glow, inner shadow, and inset.

Reflections

In this example, we're aiming to create a simple text heading that has a reflection below it and then add a little something special to the text (but very simple) to make it stand apart with very little other effects. Here's what we'll create:

1. Open a new document in Inkscape, select the Create and Edit Text tool, and enter some text. In our example, we'll use the words: `simply beautiful`

2. Next, we are going to clone the image. From the main menu select **Edit**, **Clone**, and then **Create Clone**.

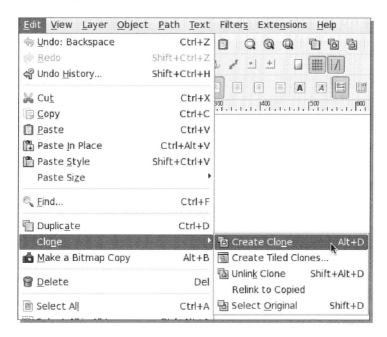

3. Now we need to flip the cloned image vertically to create the basics for our reflection. An easy way to do this is to press the *V* key (or from the main menu select **Object** and then **Flip Vertically**).

4. Move the "flipped" version below the original text.

5. From the tool box, select the rectangle tool and create a rectangle that covers the reflected (or cloned) image.

6. Since this image has the letter Y in it, and it dangles/overlaps the main text, we need to clip the text so there is no overlapping. Select this new rectangle and the text underneath it.

Or you can select the text below by using *Alt* + clicking the text's approximate location and then press *Shift* and click on Rectangle

1. From the main menu select **Object** and then **Clip** and **Set**. You'll see that the Y dangler on the reflection now doesn't exist.

2. Now create another rectangle, and cover the reflection again.

3. With the rectangle still selected, open the Fill and Stroke dialog and choose the gradient tab.

4. Set a black to white gradient on rectangle. With the gradient white on top and black at the bottom.

5. Again, select both the rectangle and the reflected text behind. Use the Select Tool, and drag around the rectangle. You should see a dotted line around the rectangle and the text behind it. Or you can select the text below by using *Alt* + clicking the text's approximate location and then press *Shift* and click on the rectangle.

6. From the main menu select **Object** and then **Mask**, and **Set**.

7. Now you have a reflection!

8. If the reflection still seems a bit dark for your taste, change the opacity in the Fill and Stroke dialog box.

9. But let's spice up this text just a little bit more. Select the first letter in each word and let's change the color—voila!

Since you cloned the image, any change you make to original text will also be changed in the reflection automatically.

6 – Using layers

When you create documents within Inskcape, you can have layers of objects. This gives great flexibility when creating graphics. You can move groups of objects on a layer, separate objects by layers (for example a background can be on one layer and a logo on another), and stack, re-order, or hide layers. The settings can be adjusted layer by layer, so you can save drafts or different versions of mockups and keep all of this in one file.

The layer you are currently using is called the drawing layer. It is selected in the Layer Dialog and is shown in a darker color.

✦ To make the Layers Dockable Dialog viewable, from the main menu select **Layer | Layers**. On the right side of your screen the Layers Dialog is displayed:

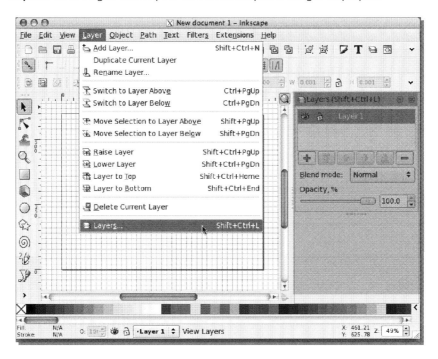

✦ You can also press *Shift + Ctrl + L* on your keyboard to display the **Layers** Dialog.

✦ In the **Layers** dialog, press the **+** button to create a new layer:

✦ In the **Layer Name** field, type a descriptive name for your graphic and click **Add**. You will notice the new layer is added above the existing one in the **Layers** dialog:

7 – Importing images

✦ Inkscape can import almost any image type—from the main menu, select **File | Import**. You can select common image file types and bring them into the open document.

✦ Or you can copy an open image and paste it into the open document, drag an image into the Inkscape canvas, or click the **Import** icon in the **Command** bar.

Any way you choose to import the images, they are only "linked" or referenced in the open document. Meaning, if you move the original file from its current location, the Inkscape file won't be able to find the image and will give you an error. But you can also embed these images into your document.

8 – Embedding images

Most imported images are only linked to the original file. If you want to embed them you need to do the following:

✦ In an open Inkscape document, select the image(s) you want to embed into the document.

✦ From the main menu select **Extensions| Images | Embed Images...**:

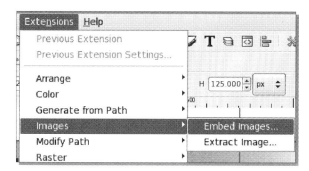

◆ Check the **Embed only selected images** box:

◆ If you want to embed all images in the document, then don't check this box.

◆ Click **Apply**.

◆ Now all images will be included within the Inkscape SVG file. This is useful if you want one all-inclusive file that can be sent or posted individually without worrying about additional source files or directory structures.

◆ Please note, however, that there are some limitations to embedding images into the Inkscape SVG files:

◇ An increase in file size. Most of the time, it can be increased by a third. (For SVG files used directly on the web, this increases bandwidth usage on the server or host).

◇ You can't share images across documents. For example, if you do one PNG image as a background file, you can't share it across SVG files.

◇ Sharing copyrighted fonts or images in a document could be illegal (depending on how extensive the rights you have purchased to use these items are to begin with). This is particularly important when working on commercial or widely used projects.

◇ If there is extensive text-editing done with the SVG files themselves, then this can be complicated and time-intensive.

People and places you should get to know

If you need help with Inkscape, here are some links to people and places which will prove invaluable.

Official sites

The site that you will find most valuable of all is, of course, the Inkscape Homepage at `http://inkscape.org/`:

It will provide you with all the manuals, current download release information, forums, and all the information about Inkscape you could want

Other important links from the official homepage are:

✦ Manual and documentation: `http://tavmjong.free.fr/INKSCAPE/MANUAL/html/index.html`

✦ Wiki: `http://wiki.inkscape.org/wiki/index.php/Inkscape`

✦ Blog: `http://planet.inkscape.org/`

✦ For developers: `https://launchpad.net/inkscape`

✦ Clip Art: `http://www.openclipart.org/`

✦ Galleries: `http://wiki.inkscape.org/wiki/index.php/Galleries`

Articles and tutorials

Inkscape has a number of official tutorials that the developers helped create that teach you about the software. You can find those here: `http://inkscape.org/doc/index.php?lang=en`.

However, you might like some other self-guided tutorials. You can find some in these locations:

✦ Inkscape Tutorials Weblog: `http://inkscapetutorials.wordpress.com/`

✦ Floss Manuals: `http://en.flossmanuals.net/Inkscape/`

✦ 10 Must-Read Inkscape Tutorials: `http://esdev.net/top-10-inkscape-tutorials/`

Community

As with many open-source programs, there are a number of mailing lists and forums you can join as a user for more resources. You can find key ones here:

- Official mailing lists: `http://inkscape.org/mailing_lists.php?lang=en`
- Official forums: `http://www.inkscapeforum.com/`
- User FAQ: `http://wiki.inkscape.org/wiki/index.php/FAQ`

Blogs

Also there are a number of blogs and screen casts (video blogs) that teach you how to use Inkscape. You can find my favorites here:

- How-To Category: Screencasters.Heathenx.org: `http://screencasters.heathenx.org/`
- Informational/How-to Category: Tavmjong Bah's Blog: `http://tavmjong.free.fr/blog/`
- Design/Graphic Category: 365 Sketches: `http://365sketches.org/`

Twitter

Here are some of the best Inkscape resources on Twitter:

- For education and tutorials:
  - The official Inkscape twitter feed: `http://twitter.com/inkscape`
  - Inkscape Tutorials: `http://twitter.com/inkscapetuts`
- For design examples:
  - FossGrafis.com : `http://twitter.com/fossgrafis`
  - Linux Artist: `http://twitter.com/linuxartist`
- For fun:
  - Inkscape Mag: `http://twitter.com/inkscapemag`
  - John Lemasney: `http://twitter.com/lemasney`
- For Open Source news:
  - `http://twitter.com/PacktOpenSource`

Index

About the author

Bethany Hiitola is a working writer and technology geek. With a degree in Scientific and Technical Communications, she's worked as a technical writer and multimedia developer for over 12 years—she spends the rest of her time as a wife, mother, gadget geek, and Master of the Household. She's written more user manuals than she can count, essays, novels, and a few technical books—including *Inkscape 0.48 Essentials for Web Designers*. More details are at her website: bethanyhiitola.com

About the Reviewer

Richard Carter is the Creative Director at Peacock Carter Ltd (http://www.peacockcarter.co.uk), a web design and development agency based in the North East of England, working with clients including Directgov, NHS Choices, and BusinessLink.

Richard is the author of *MediaWiki Skins Design*, *Magento 1.3 Themes Design*, *Joomla! 1.5 Templates Cookbook* and *Magento 1.4 Themes Design*. He has acted as a technical reviewer on *MediaWiki 1.1 Beginner's Guide*, *Inkscape 0.48 Essentials For Web Designers*, the *Definitive Guide to Drupal 7* and *Drupal 7 Business Solutions*, and is a co-founder of the Drupal North East user group (http://www.drupalnortheast.org.uk).

He blogs at http://www.earlgreyandbattenburg.co.uk and tweets nonsense at http://twitter.com/RichardCarter.

Thank you for buying
Inkscape Starter

About Packt Publishing

Packt, pronounced 'packed', published its first book "*Mastering phpMyAdmin for Effective MySQL Management*" in April 2004 and subsequently continued to specialize in publishing highly focused books on specific technologies and solutions.

Our books and publications share the experiences of your fellow IT professionals in adapting and customizing today's systems, applications, and frameworks. Our solution based books give you the knowledge and power to customize the software and technologies you're using to get the job done. Packt books are more specific and less general than the IT books you have seen in the past. Our unique business model allows us to bring you more focused information, giving you more of what you need to know, and less of what you don't.

Packt is a modern, yet unique publishing company, which focuses on producing quality, cutting-edge books for communities of developers, administrators, and newbies alike. For more information, please visit our website: www.packtpub.com.

About Packt Open Source

In 2010, Packt launched two new brands, Packt Open Source and Packt Enterprise, in order to continue its focus on specialization. This book is part of the Packt Open Source brand, home to books published on software built around Open Source licences, and offering information to anybody from advanced developers to budding web designers. The Open Source brand also runs Packt's Open Source Royalty Scheme, by which Packt gives a royalty to each Open Source project about whose software a book is sold.

Writing for Packt

We welcome all inquiries from people who are interested in authoring. Book proposals should be sent to author@packtpub.com. If your book idea is still at an early stage and you would like to discuss it first before writing a formal book proposal, contact us; one of our commissioning editors will get in touch with you.

We're not just looking for published authors; if you have strong technical skills but no writing experience, our experienced editors can help you develop a writing career, or simply get some additional reward for your expertise.

Inkscape 0.48
Illustrator's Cookbook

109 recipes to create scalable vector graphics with Inkscape

Mihaela Jurković   Rigel Di Scala

Inkscape 0.48 Illustrator's Cookbook

ISBN: 978-1-84951-266-4   Paperback: 340 pages

109 recipes to create scalable vector graphics with Inkscape

1. Create interesting illustrations and common web design elements that can be used in real-life projects

2. Gain a thorough understanding of all common Inkscape tools and advanced features of Inkscape 0.48

3. Tips and tricks to speed up your drawing workflow

Inkscape 0.48
Essentials for Web Designers

Use the fascinating Inkscape graphics editor to create attractive layout designs, images, and icons for your website

Bethany Hiitola   PACKT open source*

Inkscape 0.48 Essentials for Web Designers

ISBN: 978-1-84951-268-8   Paperback: 316 pages

Use the fascinating Inkscape graphics editor to create attractive layout designs, images, and icons for your website

1. The first book on the newly released Inkscape version 0.48, with an exclusive focus on web design

2. Comprehensive coverage of all aspects of Inkscape required for web design

3. Incorporate eye-catching designs, patterns, and other visual elements to spice up your web pages

Please check **www.PacktPub.com** for information on our titles

Made in the USA
Columbia, SC
07 January 2020